A JOURNEY
through the

Peak
District

Introduction

*All Derbyshire is full of steep hills, and nothing but
the peakes of hills as thick one by another is seen in most
of the County which are very steepe.*

This is how pioneering travel writer Celia Fiennes described a journey through the Peak District in 1697. The Peak District, however, is not confined to Derbyshire. It stretches from Huddersfield in the north almost as far as Derby in the south, spilling over into neighbouring Staffordshire, Greater Manchester, Cheshire, and south and west Yorkshire. The word 'Peak' derives from *peac*, the old English word for 'hill'. The region was first called Peac-land in Anglo-Saxon times, when the local tribe were know as the Pecsaetan, or peak-dwellers.

Surrounded by the industrial conurbations of the southern Pennines and the Midlands, the Peak District has long been a welcome green 'lung' for urban workers. In the 1920s and '30s it became the main battleground for the access to the countryside movement. At that time many of the highest and wildest moors, such as Kinder Scout and Bleaklow, were kept by land-owners and gamekeepers for grouse-shooting, and walkers were prohibited. Direct action was taken by the ramblers with the famous Mass Trespass of 24 April 1932, which acted as an important catalyst for the development of the National

Parks after World War II. The Peak District was the first National Park to be designated, in 1951.

Within the 555 sq miles (1,437 sq km) of the Peak District National Park there are vast contrasts in the landscape. The 'White Peak' of the south encompasses steep-sided, wooded limestone gorges and bright green fields criss-crossed by drystone walls. It is also the setting for idyllic, unspoilt villages. In comparison, the gritstone of the Dark Peak to the north has a rugged, austere beauty. Its lonely, windswept moorlands evoke the 'howling wilderness' that the intrepid traveller Daniel Defoe described in the early 18th century.

Much of the region was converted into a hunting ground under the Normans, when the Royal Forest of the Peak was governed from Peveril Castle, above Castleton. Wealth generated from sheep-farming and lead- and copper-mining over the centuries is reflected in the Peak District's fine historic buildings. Haddon Hall, Chatsworth, and the Duke of Devonshire's elegant Crescent in Buxton, modelled on Bath's Royal Crescent, are particularly worthy of a visit.

The Peak District was also a cradle of the Industrial Revolution. Sir Richard Arkwright established the world's first successful water-powered cotton mill at Cromford, starting an inexorable trend. Today, though, the Peak District is a peaceful haven away from the noise and bustle of modern life. It is the only British National Park to be awarded the Council of Europe's Diploma for Nature Conservation – a distinction it has held for more than thirty years and a measure of its success in protecting the unique human and natural resources of the area.

Autumn view from Treak Cliff, near Castleton

Northern Peak District

The so-called 'Dark Peak' consists mainly of gritstone, also known as millstone grit because it was used to grind corn in mills. The moorlands, stripped of tree cover, are bleak and windswept, covered only by thin soil, mosses and heather. Higher up, the landscape changes to peat bogs, split into channels called 'groughs'. The extraordinary silhouettes of gritstone tors, shaped by constant exposure to the elements, are often the only landmarks on the horizon.

The wild, seemingly inhospitable moorland of the Dark Peak nevertheless bears traces of human activity from ancient times. Carl Wark, near Hathersage, for example, probably dates from the Iron Age, and there are remains of an even earlier hill fort on the summit of Mam Tor.

At Doctor's Gate near Snake Pass, a well-preserved section of Roman road survives.

Man's intervention on the landscape was more dramatic in the 20th century, when valleys were flooded to create reservoirs of drinking-water for the rapidly expanding cities of Derby, Nottingham, Sheffield and Leicester. However, the reservoirs at Howden, Ladybower and

Isolated farm in
the Dark Peak

Derwent now blend into the natural landscape and are popular with both birdwatchers and anglers.

The landscape of the northern Peak poses exciting challenges to walkers. Many stop to eat or rest at Edale at the start of the Pennine Way, near the base of Kinder Scout. For the less-active visitor there are the delights of exploring villages such as Hathersage, the awesome caves around Castleton, or the classical splendour of Lyme Hall.

1 The view from Snake Pass towards Glossop. Completed in 1821, Snake Pass is one of the most famous roads in Britain. It runs between Sheffield and Glossop, reaching a height of 1,680 ft (512m). The name is derived from the crest of the Devonshire family, major local landowners.

2 There is a well-preserved section of Roman road at Doctor's Gate (right), near the Snake Pass Inn.

3 Glossop (right) is the western gateway to the Peak District. With its swift-flowing streams and proximity to Manchester, it developed into a thriving cotton-manufacturing town. The 17th-century cottages next to the church in Old Glossop evoke the village before the Industrial Revolution.

4 Derwent Reservoir was used for practice runs for the famous 617 Squadron 'Dambusters' raid on Germany during World War II. It was also the location for the classic film.

5 Howden, Derwent and Ladybower (pictured) reservoirs form one of the largest man-made areas of water in Europe.

6 Howden Reservoir. The high rainfall and topography of the upper Derwent valley made it ideal for building dams in the late 19th century to supply drinking-water for the growing cities of Derby, Nottingham, Leicester and Sheffield.

7 Holmfirth is the setting for the popular television series *Last of the Summer Wine*. As well as exploring the picturesque narrow alleys, weavers' cottages and postcard museum, visitors can call at Nora Batty's House or Sid's Café.

8 A selection of cafés, pubs and guesthouses caters for ramblers in Edale.

9 Grindsbrook Booth is the main settlement in Edale and a major walking centre.

10 The first stretch of the Pennine Way, from Edale across Kinder, Bleaklow and Black Hill, is considered to be the toughest.

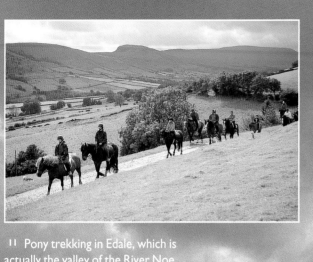

12 Edale is a starting point for the Pennine Way, the 250-mile (400km) route up the spine of England to the Scottish borders.

11 Pony trekking in Edale, which is actually the valley of the River Noe and the five hamlets or booths (cattle shelters) within it.

13 Mam Tor is known as the 'Shivering Mountain' because of the instability of its lower layers. The loose, soft shales are constantly crumbling away, giving the impression that the hill is trembling.

14 Kinder Downfall is on the western edge of the Kinder Scout plateau, the highest point in the Dark Peak at 2,088 ft (636m).

15 Winnats Pass is the only direct route between Castleton and the west for motorists. The spectacular gorge is thought to be have been created by the waters of a huge lagoon, possibly released by an earthquake.

16 Kinder Scout is furrowed by deep groughs or peat gullies.

17 The 50-ft (15m) high entrance to Peak Cavern is beneath the hill on which Peveril Castle stands. The cave has been known to tourists for hundreds of years.

18 Visitors may walk for a mile underground, and see the 100-ft high Great Cave, which descends to the River Styx, once thought to be the entrance to Hades.

20 Treak Cliff Cavern is famous for the stalactites and stalagmites in the Dream (pictured) and Aladdin caves, as well as for its veins of Blue John. In the 'Dome of St Paul's' cave the ceiling is 40 ft (12m) high and ablaze with colour.

21 This Blue John table, in the Ollerenshaw Collection at Castleton, came from the Treak Cliff workings, the only viable source of the beautiful, banded mineral today.

19 Castleton is surrounded by a mixture of natural caves and caverns created by mining for lead and other minerals. The Peak, Blue John, Treak Cliff and Speedwell caverns are the most spectacular.

22 Peveril Castle was founded in 1086 by William Peverel, an illegitimate son of William the Conqueror. Sir Walter Scott's novel *Peveril of the Peak* was inspired by the Peverel family. The great keep was built by Henry II in 1176.

23 Hope was once an important centre of the Royal Forest of the Peak, the hunting ground of successive medieval kings. This Saxon cross stands in its churchyard.

24 Abandoned millstones on Stanage Edge. Stanage is the most famous of the Peak District 'edges' – the series of steep, gritstone escarpments that overlook the Derwent valley.

25 Little John, the right-hand man of the legendary Robin Hood, is believed to be buried in Hathersage village churchyard.

26 Charlotte Brontë once stayed at Hathersage ('Heather's Edge') and used the name of the local lords of the manor – the Eyres – for her famous heroine.

27 Carl Wark, seen here from Higger Tor, is an ancient hill fort.

28 Open moorland and gritstone outcrops characterise the landscape beyond Hathersage, typified by Burbage Rocks and Hathersage Moor.

29 There are superb views from Higger Tor, near Hathersage, including the ancient fortification of Carl Wark to the east, Stanage Edge to the north, and the River Derwent to the west.

30 Burbage Brook runs through beautiful Padley Gorge, one of the few places in the Peak District where ancient woodland survives. It is part of Longshaw Country Park, a National Trust property.

31 Lyme Park belonged to the Legh family for nearly 600 years, before it became a National Trust property in 1946. It featured in the latest television adaptation of Jane Austen's *Pride and Prejudice*. The elegant south front was built by the Italian architect Leoni in the 18th century.

Southern Peak District

The 'White Peak' of the southern Peak District is essentially a limestone plateau divided by the valleys of the rivers Manifold, Dove, Lathkill and Wye. During the Ice Age, swollen by melt-water from glaciers, these rivers cut almost perpendicular gorges through the rock. The bright white limestone that gives the area its name can be seen on the edges of these gorges. Another characteristic landscape feature are the isolated 'needles' of more resistant limestones, such as Tissington Spires, Ilam Rock and Pickering Tor in Dove Dale.

Dove Dale is perhaps the best-known and most visited of the White Peak dales, but they are all wildlife havens. Lathkill Dale, for example, with its clear waters and ash woodland, supports a wide range of aquatic and bird life, as well as many rare species of wildflowers.

The porous limestone of the White Peak accounts for the area's fantastic natural caves, such as Poole's Cavern at Buxton, where the rock has been eroded by water. Buxton is the largest town in the Peak District, and was first

exploited as a spa by the Romans. In the 18th and 19th centuries both Buxton and Matlock were developed as inland resorts.

Prosperous local landowning families built two of the Peak District's finest historic houses in the southern Peak District: romantic Haddon Hall, an unspoilt manor house that has been the seat of the Manners family (earls and later dukes of Rutland) since 1558, and Chatsworth, the palatial home of the Duke of Devonshire.

Matlock Bath
from Riber Castle

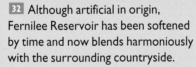

32 Although artificial in origin, Fernilee Reservoir has been softened by time and now blends harmoniously with the surrounding countryside.

33 The damming of the River Goyt in the 20th century created Fernilee and Errwood (pictured) reservoirs in 1938 and 1967 respectively.

34 Buxton's opulent Edwardian Opera House has now been restored to its former glory. Built in 1905, it hosts productions throughout the year and is the main venue for the festival of arts and music held each July.

35 Buxton is an elegant spa town with a number of fine buildings ranging from Georgian to Edwardian times, when its popularity was at a peak. The Romans first discovered its mineral-rich waters, and in medieval times the springs were dedicated to St Ann. Mary Queen of Scots visited in 1573 in search of a cure for her rheumatism.

36 Buxton's Pavilion overlooks pleasant gardens.

38 The show cave at Poole's Cavern, Buxton, has amazing rock formations, brilliantly illuminated.

37 The 18th-century Crescent, built by John Carr of York, was designed to include a town house for the Duke of Devonshire (at the centre, bearing his coat of arms).

39 With its distinctive peak, Shutlingsloe has been described as the 'Cheshire Matterhorn'. It stands 1,659 ft (506m) high, with panoramic views from the summit including the Macclesfield Forest and the Cheshire Plain.

40 The rivers Dove, Manifold, Wye, Derwent and Goyt begin their journey to the sea from the bleak expanses of Axe Edge Moor. The watery slopes rise to more than 1,800 ft (540m) before ending abruptly at Axe Edge.

41 A winter scene near Flash, said to be the highest village in England, standing at 1,518 ft (462m).

42 The drystone walls of the Peak District vary in composition. These white and grey limestone walls near Sheldon divide fields in the White Peak. In a gritstone area the rocks are darker and flatter.

43 In the evening light Ramshaw Rocks create an evocative silhouette on the skyline.

44 Hen Cloud from the Roaches. The name probably derives from the French *roche*, or rock.

45 The Roaches provide a wonderful viewpoint for walkers and a wide choice of pitches for climbers.

46 Ramshaw Rocks are part of the rocky western arm of the gritstone horseshoe that surrounds the White Peak.

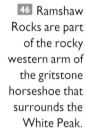

47 Eyam Hall dates from 1676 and is open to the public. The manor house was the home of the Wright family for more than 300 years.

49 The Great Plague of London spread to Eyam in September 1665 – possibly via cloth ordered from the capital by George Viccars, a local tailor. Within a year 260 of the 350 villagers had died. The Plague Cottage by the church was the lodgings of Viccars, the first victim.

48 Eyam village contains many poignant reminders of the Great Plague, including the Riley Graves – commemorating seven members of one family who died in the space of eight days.

50 Tideswell's imposing 14th-century parish church is nicknamed the 'Cathedral of the Peak'. It was built at a time when Tideswell was an important market town and lead-mining centre, hence its grandeur.

51 Ashford in the Water is an attractive village of mainly 18th- and 19th-century limestone cottages. The picturesque three-arched packhorse bridge over the River Wye is known as the Sheepwash Bridge, because at shearing time sheep were kept in the enclosure next to it before they were washed in the river.

52 Magpie Mine, situated near Sheldon, is the Peak District's best-preserved lead mine. Now a field study centre, it was worked for 230 years and its twin chimneys (the square one built by local miners, the round one by Cornishmen) form a distinctive landmark.

54 When the railway closed, part of the track was bought by the National Park and became the Monsal Trail, a footpath and cycle track. The viaduct is now a listed structure.

53 John Ruskin was incensed when the high viaduct spanning Monsal Dale was built to carry the Manchester–Derby railway in the 19th century, declaring: 'Now, every fool in Buxton can be at Bakewell in half-an-hour, and every fool in Bakewell at Buxton, which you think a lucrative process of exchange – you Fools Everywhere!'

55 Monsal Dale is one of the beauty spots of the Peak District

56 A huge solitary boulder called the Eagle Stone stands on Baslow Edge.

57 Heather-clad open moorland ends dramatically at the crags of Froggat Edge.

58 A magnificent gritstone escarpment stretches along the eastern edge of the Derwent valley. It offers exhilarating walking and glorious views, as seen here from Curbar Edge.

59 Bakewell's parish church of All Saints contains several Saxon carvings, and two Saxon preaching crosses in the churchyard.

60 Bakewell's varied past as a market town, short-lived spa and textile centre is reflected in an intriguing blend of architecture, dating from the 16th to the 19th century. The town's history is told at the Old House Museum.

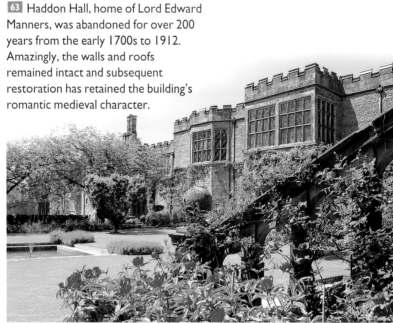

63 Haddon Hall, home of Lord Edward Manners, was abandoned for over 200 years from the early 1700s to 1912. Amazingly, the walls and roofs remained intact and subsequent restoration has retained the building's romantic medieval character.

61 Bakewell is the natural 'capital' of the Peak District. An important tourist base, it is famed for its egg and jam 'puddings'. The magnificent bridge over the River Wye dates from the 13th century.

64 Edensor was built by the 6th Duke of Devonshire between 1838 and 1842, to replace the original settlement which obscured his view over the park from Chatsworth.

62 Chatsworth was built between 1686 and 1707 for William Cavendish, the 1st Duke of Devonshire. The 290-ft (88m) Emperor Fountain was built in honour of a visit from the Tsar of Russia that never materialised. 'Capability' Brown straightened the river in the 18th century to create the parkland's sweeping lawns and picturesque tree groupings.

65 Picturesque Conksbury Bridge spans the River Lathkill near Youlgreave.

66 The enigmatic stone circle at Arbor Low, near Monyash, is known as the 'Stonehenge of the Peak'. It dates from around 2000 BC and was probably used for religious rituals in the Bronze Age.

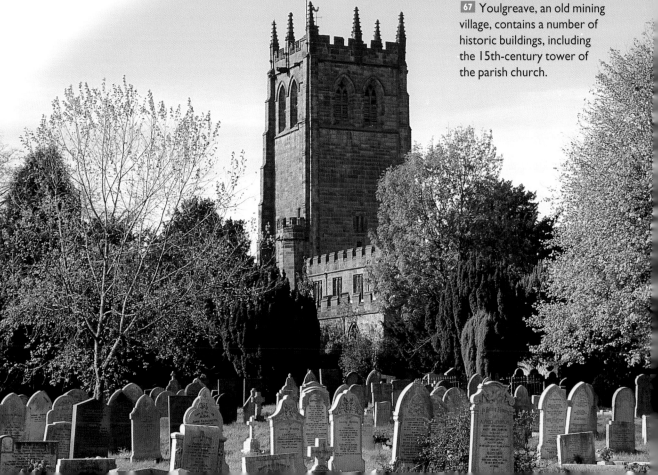

67 Youlgreave, an old mining village, contains a number of historic buildings, including the 15th-century tower of the parish church.

68 Nine Ladies stone circle on Stanton Moor also dates from the Bronze Age. Its size, 50 ft (15m) across, indicates it may once have been a burial ground of some importance.

69 Lathkill Dale is the site of a nature reserve. Many different species of plants, including the midnight blue Jacob's Ladder, a national rarity, can be found here.

70 Further up Lathkill Dale the pure, clean water of the river drops over weirs and falls.

71 Matlock Bath is an extension of Matlock, which became a popular spa resort in the 19th century after the construction of a road and railway through Derwent Gorge. Cable cars now cross the gorge to the Heights of Abraham, where visitors can enjoy views reminiscent of the Swiss Alps on a fine day.

72 The River Derwent at Matlock Bath is a popular venue for canoeists.

73 The largest of the 'hydropathic establishments' or hydros, built for visitors to take the spa waters at Matlock Bath, now serves as council offices.

74 Lead-mining in the area has a 2,500-year-old history, which is described in the Peak District Mining Museum at Matlock Bath Pavilion.

75 Many of the original mill buildings at Cromford remain, painstakingly restored as craft units and shops by the Arkwright Society. The canal, which was opened in 1793 and closed in 1944, has now been restored for pleasure trips.

76 Sir Richard Arkwright established the first successful water-powered cotton mill at Cromford in 1771, starting the transformation of textile manufacturing from a cottage-based to a factory-based industry.

77 The story of the Cromford and High Peak Railway is told at the visitor centre at Middleton Top Engine House.

78 Wirksworth appears to have been an important lead-mining centre in Roman times. A Saxon carving in the church shows a lead-miner setting off for work with a pickaxe and basket.

79 Peak Rail steam train services recommenced between Matlock and Darley Dale (pictured) in 1991.

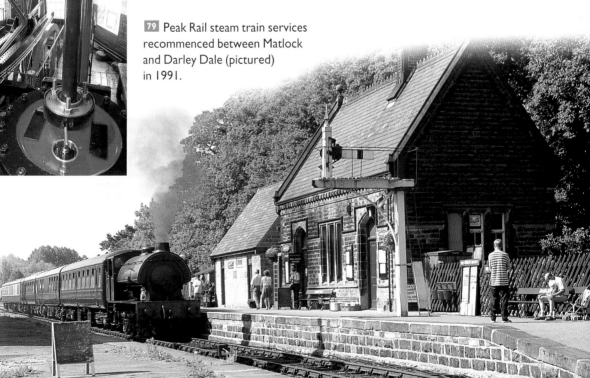

80 Manifold Valley scene. The River Manifold flows roughly parallel to the Dove, with many twists and turns, true to its name.

81 Hartington is famous for producing Stilton cheese, using milk from Peak District dairy farms. The former market town contains a handsome medieval church and a number of limestone houses, inns and shops grouped round a spacious square.

82 From the great yawning gap of Thor's Cave there are breath-taking views up the Manifold Valley. Evidence of prehistoric occupation of the cave has been unearthed.

83 Near Hartington the River Dove flows through the narrow, steep-sided Wolfscote Dale (pictured). Izaak Walton and Charles Cotton, authors of *The Compleat Angler*, frequently fished in this area, describing the Dove as 'the princess of rivers'.

84 Jesse Watts Russell, a wealthy industrialist, rebuilt Ilam Hall in the Gothic style of the 1820s. He resited Ilam village, remodelled in a unique Alpine style, out of sight of the hall in the 1850s.

85 From the stepping-stones beneath Thorpe Cloud, Dove Dale is 7 miles (11km) in length. The valley's name changes successively to Milldale, Wolfscote Dale and Beresford Dale before the Dove reaches Hartington.

86 Ilam Country Hall Park is in the care of the National Trust and open to the public.

87 Dove Dale is one of the most scenic valleys in England. Izaak Walton and Charles Cotton described the wonderful fishing in the area in *The Compleat Angler*, a guide first published in 1653.

88 The limestone ravine is overhung with a series of dramatic crags, caves and pinnacles, including Ilam Rock.

89 The Georgian market town of Ashbourne describes itself as 'the gateway to Dove Dale'. The Tudor Grammar School dates from 1585.

90 Well-dressing is believed to date back to the time of the Black Death, in the middle of the 14th century, as a form of thanksgiving for the purity of the well water. The tradition was revived in Tissington in 1615, when the wells did not run dry despite a severe drought.

91 Tissington has a strong well-dressing tradition. Each year, on Ascension Day, the village wells are decorated with tableaux of flowers, ferns, mosses, leaves and bark which are pressed on to wooden frames covered with clay.